50 KINDNESS ACTIVITIES

FOR

PARENTS

ELYSE MILLER

50 Kindness Activities for Parents

© Copyright 2024 Focus Five Group

ISBN: 978-1-9990313-4-3

For copies or press, please contact
sales@kindnessforsuccessbyDJR.com

Kindness Activities for Parents

Teaching children kindness from a young age can lead not only to increased empathy and compassion but also to their own eventual intrinsic success as research shows that kindness often leads to success in the workplace, in academics, in relationships and in life.

1

Teach children about common human-ity. What does that mean? Dr. Kristen Neff notes that this is a process whereby we acknowledge that we all share the same feelings and emotions and that we are all on a common journey through-out life. Teaching children about our world and about different cultures can expand their tolerance levels and increase their understanding that we're all fallible.

2

Remember that children learn what they live. You are their role models. Model kind behaviour.

3

Feel free to show affection with a happy smile and hugs daily offering acceptance of your child as they are. This can help them to accept themselves, which in turn, will aid them in navigating their lives as adults. Each child is unique. Embrace their differences.

4

Showing family camaraderie can ensure strong family ties. Plan fun family outings where everyone is involved, and everyone can suggest a place to visit next.

5

Actively listen to your child so that you know his social environment well. Is he or she treated with respect in schools and other environments? If not, can you both devise a plan to change this?

6

Show your child appreciation for their acts of kindness. Show them appreciation for their effort in their schoolwork and extra-curricular activities or their eagerness to help others, including their siblings.

7

Encourage effort on your child's part by using positive reinforcement. What is their favorite thing to do? Or utilize a trip to the nearest toy store.

8

Point out each child's unique capability and allow the child to use their unique talent to help the family.

9

Write your child a note to express your appreciation for all that they do. Elaborate on their strengths and encourage their success by noting what they are most capable of.

10

Let your child help you
cook their favorite
meal. Let your child
help you cook meals
for other members
of the family.

11

Speak kindly of others and encourage your child to speak kindly of others too. Help them to see those they interact with in a positive light.

12

Set a day for cleaning where each child can take a task to ensure clothes and toys are put away. Each child can perform the cleaning task they enjoy most. One child can sweep the floor, while another child can clear the table, while another can clean cabinets or put away toys. Reward them for Cleaning Day with a fun family outing.

13

Forest Therapy is healing. Walks in nearby treed parks can be calming and a creative way to not only get fresh air, but also sunlight (Vitamin D).

14

Encourage gratitude by asking "What makes you happy? Babysamanddad on TikTok use this phrase regularly on their father and son skits and this type of question encourages children to look at the cup half full. As in Positive Psychology, train your children to see what is right, not what is wrong.

15

You can create a Family Gratitude Day when everyone writes what they are particularly grateful for that day, and this can be shared during a family meal.

16

Ask your child about his or her future goals and dreams. What do they like to do best? How do they see themselves in the future? What small steps can be made to achieve these goals? Once these small steps are achieved, celebrate the achievement.

17

Teach your children to plant indoor or outdoor plants. Teach them how to care for plants and watch them grow together.

18

All feelings can be discussed, acknowledged, and accepted. But emotions from the "dark side" as positive psychology refers to negative emotions need to be controlled after acknowledgement. Ways to acknowledge and deal with emotions from the "dark side" can include writing therapy by encouraging children to write about their negative emotions for at least ten minutes. Or alternatively, if the child is young, art therapy can be used. They can draw, colour, or paint their negative feelings. Once relieved, the writing and drawing can be thrown out indicating that it is time to move forward.

19

Point out the positives in your child, their siblings, teachers, and peers. This can be done with occasional notes. Encourage them to see the positive in everyone they encounter.

20

Participate in charity events as a family or volunteer as a family for a community event.

21

Encourage your child to learn to share by having them exchange a favorite toy with his or her friend for a week.

22

Participate in a communal activity such as gathering donations to feed the homeless or hungry. Or organize lemonade stands for charity. Or participate in a food or toy drive particularly during holidays where each child can donate canned food or a toy they no longer play with or that they may want to buy from their allowance.

23

Create a community social media page with your children's writing or art and encourage all members to like each other's posts.

24

Read positive news online together to encourage your child not only to know the world around them, but also to debate their ideas about world events.

25

Help your child create a photo album of all the positive events in their life. Bring a camera to family outings or friend events.

26

Play with your child. Enjoy online games and board games together.

27

Debates stimulate critical thinking at all ages. Engage children in debates when appropriate.

28

Share interesting videos and discuss the content, particularly videos that discuss and promote kindness. Ask your child what they think about the video.

29

Teach your children how to be empathic by showing your own concern for others and engaging in acts of kindness.

30

Have a piggy bank that you give to charities and encourage your child to give.

31

Read kindness and anti-bullying books together with your child. Discuss their
meaning and how they feel about the book.
What do they think about the book's message? Does the kindness message come
across well?

32

Put out a Kindness Actions Jar in the kitchen where you can put in some coins anytime a kindness action takes place. Later you can all decide what to do with the money, whether it be a family outing or a trip to the toy store.

33

During the holidays or at the beginning or end of the school year, encourage your child to write their teacher a note of kindness showing appreciation for all they do.

34

Encourage your child to help others do homework or to do research with a friend.

35

Have an exploratory family outing to a museum or a historic home. Learning how people lived in past generations without heat, electricity, telephones, or transportation can increase empathy and gratitude.

36

Do a 1000-piece puzzle together or encourage your child to complete a puzzle with a friend, taking the time to enjoy the process.

37

Teach your children that united we stand, divided we fall. Staying united through compromise and understanding brings increased success.

38

Add a few sealed snacks in your child's lunchbox they can share with friends, if allowed by their school.

39

Create a family mural about kindness and place it where everyone can see it.

40

Encourage your child to write and draw a story about kindness that he can read regularly.

41

Find a fun exercise activity like biking or dancing you all like to do together and set a regular weekly time to do it.

42

In warmer weather, play a sport like floor hockey, baseball, basketball, or soccer together as a family.

43

Encourage your child to shake hands with the opposing team before any sports event to encourage camaraderie rather than competition.

44

Plan a singing or theatrical event for your child and his or her friends. They can write a script and/or songs about kindness and perform it for the parents.

45

Have your children do the The Character Strengths Inventory for Children (CSI-C) to understand themselves better and to help them learn about their strengths. Discuss how they can best utilize their strengths for themselves and in interaction with others.

46

Make up a family medley such as "I wish you sunshine everyday, may all the best things come your way and ever since that you were born, you brought us sunshine every morn," (tune from 1988 Kellogg's Corn Flakes - Our Best To You Each Morn). Use a familiar tune or your own tune.

47

Let your child add their input to an upcoming trip with their own itinerary for a day or two of your planned vacation. Often children come up with very interesting places to visit.

48

Teach your child to enjoy the moment. To take the time to absorb experiences and to feel their emotions, but to find positive outlets for all feelings. What can be done to change this negative moment, if one exists, to a positive one?

49

Discuss kindness activities your child performed at school or after school during family meetings or at mealtimes. How did these activities make them feel?

50

Utilize a Kindness Contest where each child performs a kindness activity and gets points for each kindness action performed. At the end of the week, the child with the most points can decide where they would like their next family outing to be.

Kindness in the family is a platform for kindness within humanity. Kindness in the home grows into kindness for other peoples and environments.

These activities were designed to enhance the parental and family bond while developing a culture of kindness. Role modelling kindness can extend within all environments and thereby worldwide.

www.ingramcontent.com/pod-product-compliance
Lightning Source LLC
Chambersburg PA
CBHW061325120626
46546CB00007B/2675